Matthew Mouse

A story based on Proverbs

Written and illustrated by Zoe Carter

Copyright Zoe Carter 2017

The Bible is a great big library. Sixty-six
books in all. Some are big and some are small.

Books about the past, books about the future, letters, poems, stories that are true. And all the books are from God to you.

Let's have a look at the book of Proverbs.

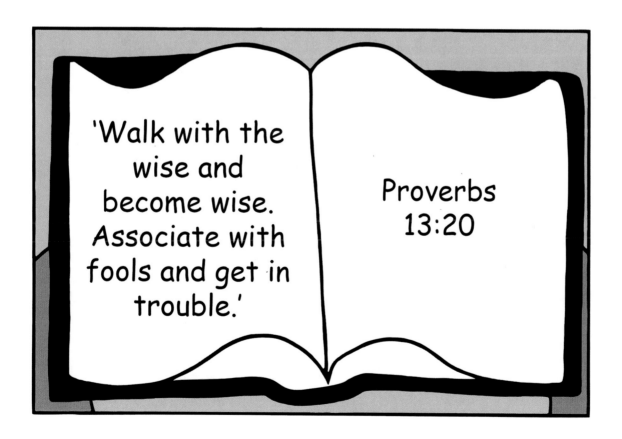

'Walk with the wise and become wise. Associate with fools and get in trouble.'

Proverbs 13:20

'I don't understand', said Little Owl.

'Sometimes the best way to understand a difficult idea is to tell a good story...'

Matthew Mouse looked at a poster. He looked and he thought and he thought some more.

'Be a friend to everyone. That sounds exciting.
That sounds fun.'

Matthew was becoming terribly bored with playing
with Melissa moose.

So he was very interested to meet a new friend,
the cat burglar.

'Come and play with me', said the cat burglar. 'It will be so much fun.'

And Matthew did. He played with him all day.

And he played with him all night.

And the more he played with him, the more he became like him.

He started to dress like him.

And he started to behave like him.

Even if Matthew Mouse hadn't actually done anything...

he would be blamed for trouble just by being seen next to the cat burglar.

But the games started to become more dangerous.
'Help me break into this house', said the cat burglar.

'I can't do that. What if we get caught?' answered
Matthew.

'I thought you were my friend.' said the cat burglar.
'Friends help each other.'

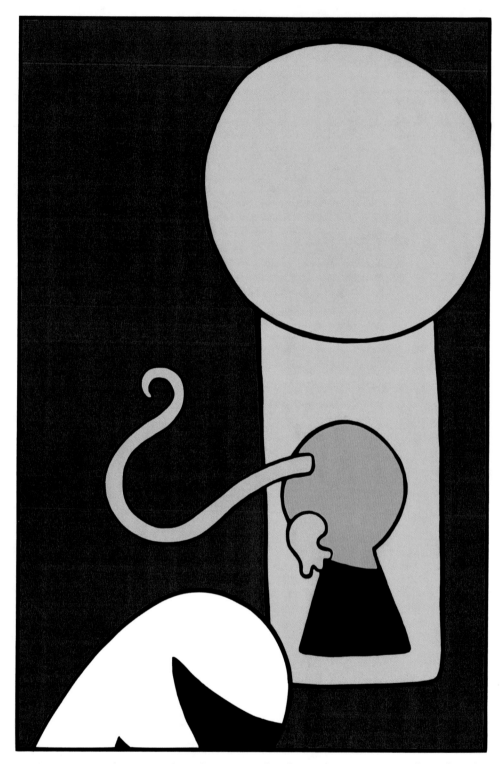

'Climb in through the keyhole and open the lock from the inside', the cat burglar said to Matthew.

Matthew wanted to be a good friend, so he did what the cat burglar said.

'Help me! I'm stuck', Matthew cried out.
But the cat burglar didn't care. He ran away as
fast as he could.

PC Panda was on patrol. He pulled Matthew out of the keyhole. 'Matthew!' he exclaimed in shock. 'What were you doing in there? That is not your house. This is not like you!'

'Please don't arrest me', said Matthew. 'The cat burglar told me to. I was just trying to help him. I was trying to be a good friend. We are supposed to be friends with everyone.'

'I disagree', said PC Panda. 'We should be kind to everyone, but we need to pick our friends very carefully.'

'Here, let me change this poster.'

Matthew never forgot the trouble the cat burglar
got him into. He realised Melissa was a good friend,
so he played with her instead.

When he saw that the cat burglar needed help, he would help him.

But when the cat burglar wanted to play, Matthew would run far far away.

So when trouble finally caught up with the cat burglar...

Matthew Mouse was nowhere to be found.

The End

'Nothing will make God love you more, and nothing will make God love you less. Proverbs teaches us to be wise, so that we can know how to live and make good choices.

Zoe Carter lives in Edinburgh, the capital of Scotland. She loves to make puppets, drink tea with her friends, and dress up in fancy dress costumes. Her favourite animal is an octopus.

www.zoecraftbook.com

Check out Zoe's Bible craft activity website www.zoecraftbook.com
More than 100 craft activities with full step by step photographic
instructions and templates. Fun, high quality and easy. Suitable for boys
and girls. Ideal for Sunday school, church, holiday clubs, homeschooling,
family time, VBS, camps, away days and many more.

Other titles by Zoe Carter

And many more

Available now from Amazon

Made in the USA
Las Vegas, NV
23 December 2023

83444391R00021